The Red Squirrels of Bro

Introduction

We hope you enjoy our little book, which is an intimate snapshot of one of our most endearing creatures.

It is said that what we eat is what we are: for that reason the Scots Pine is very important to the red squirrel, as seeds, or pine nuts as they are also called, are available nearly all year. This is especially true on Brownsea Island. The red squirrel, a mammal, is native to Britain and is cute to look at, but what else do we know about this shy creature?

The whole of Britain was once home to our native red squirrel, but is this still true today?

The following pages answer those questions and many others: but as well as talking specifically about the red squirrels of Brownsea Island, we need to mention the grey squirrel, which, although it does not reside on Brownsea Island, has had a big impact on the red squirrel's life on the mainland.

A third of the book follows the red squirrel's progress through the centuries; with two thirds concentrating on the red squirrels of Brownsea Island.

The Introduction of the Red Squirrel to Britain

When the red squirrel first appeared, Britain was not an island, as it was joined to Europe. The red squirrel had also colonised Ireland at this time, which was just before the last Ice Age, when the continents of Africa and Europe collided, resulting in massive earth movements.

Red squirrels seem to have flourished from the twelfth century onwards, although during the sixteenth century their numbers began declining in Scotland, where, in the eighteenth century they became extinct. This decline seems to be mainly because of loss of habitat due to changes in agriculture. When replanting took place during the nineteenth century the red squirrels were reintroduced to Scotland, where a hundred years later they were abundant.

The red squirrel population in Ireland seems to have suffered similar changes over the centuries.

By the end of the fifteenth century, red squirrels were extinct in Ireland, yet only one hundred years earlier they were so prolific, and the trees so thick, it was said that a squirrel could travel across a whole county without touching the ground.

By the twentieth century the red squirrels were a common sight in the British Isles and were often destroyed on a large scale, being thought of as forest pests.

Alas, another decline followed.

Although numbers were affected in the conifer forests of Wales, Scotland and Ireland, this decline has been most devastating during the latter half of the twentieth century in the English deciduous woods.

3

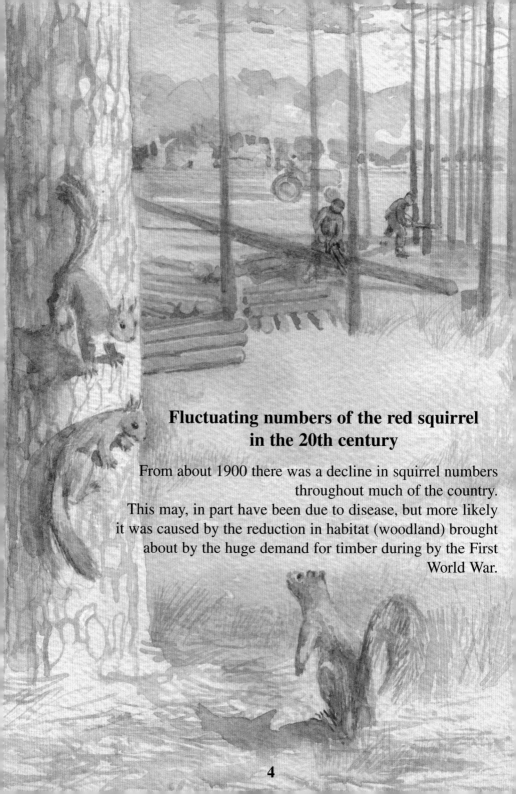

Fluctuating numbers of the red squirrel
in the 20th century

From about 1900 there was a decline in squirrel numbers
throughout much of the country.
This may, in part have been due to disease, but more likely
it was caused by the reduction in habitat (woodland) brought
about by the huge demand for timber during by the First
World War.

In spite of this, by the 1930s numbers increased again in some areas of the country, although never reaching pre 1900 levels. In other areas the grey squirrel was now well established, thus preventing a widespread return by the red squirrel.

As recently as 1970 the red squirrel was common in East Anglia, Northern England and Wales, but sadly over the past forty years there has been a dramatic decline throughout England and Wales.

Although the loss of woodland habitat has certainly contributed to the decline of the red squirrel, the introduction of the grey squirrel (Sciurus carolinensis) from North America to Britain in 1876 is thought to be also responsible.

The disease, Parapoxvirus, (now known as squirrel pox virus), which 60% of the greys carry, reached epidemic proportions in areas where the red squirrel declined.

Although found in the rest of Europe, red squirrels are an endangered species in Britain.

Not long ago they were found all over the country; sadly in Britain today there are approximately 160,000 red squirrels as opposed to 2.5 million greys.

Apart from Brownsea Island, the red squirrels can be seen on the Isle of Wight; Formby near Liverpool; Northumberland; Scotland and more closely on Furzey Island in Poole harbour, where around forty red squirrels live since being imported from Wales.

Interestingly, 75% of the British population of red squirrels live in Scotland.

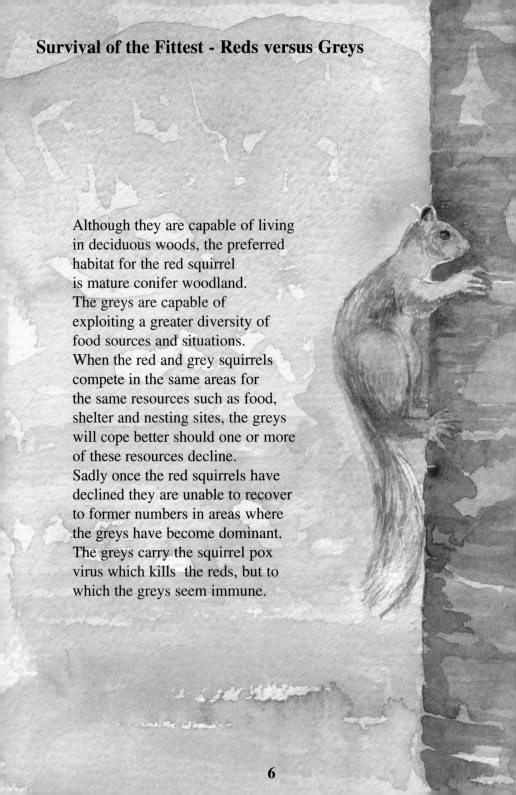

Survival of the Fittest - Reds versus Greys

Although they are capable of living
in deciduous woods, the preferred
habitat for the red squirrel
is mature conifer woodland.
The greys are capable of
exploiting a greater diversity of
food sources and situations.
When the red and grey squirrels
compete in the same areas for
the same resources such as food,
shelter and nesting sites, the greys
will cope better should one or more
of these resources decline.
Sadly once the red squirrels have
declined they are unable to recover
to former numbers in areas where
the greys have become dominant.
The greys carry the squirrel pox
virus which kills the reds, but to
which the greys seem immune.

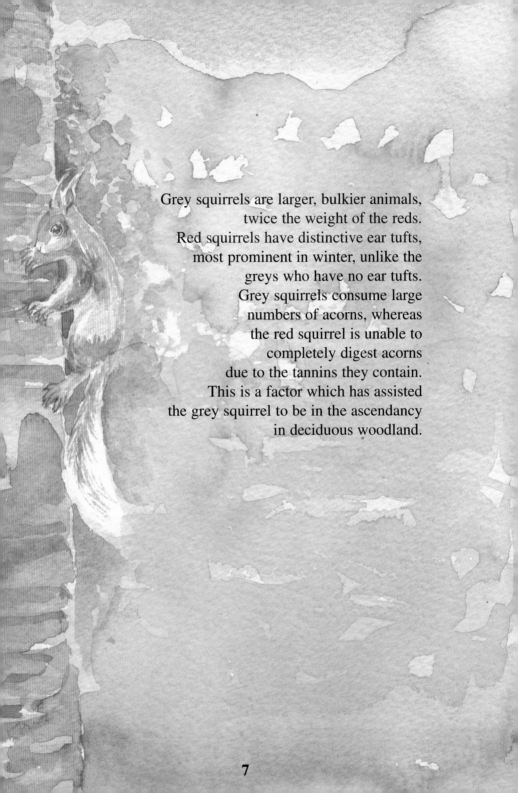

Grey squirrels are larger, bulkier animals,
twice the weight of the reds.
Red squirrels have distinctive ear tufts,
most prominent in winter, unlike the
greys who have no ear tufts.
Grey squirrels consume large
numbers of acorns, whereas
the red squirrel is unable to
completely digest acorns
due to the tannins they contain.
This is a factor which has assisted
the grey squirrel to be in the ascendancy
in deciduous woodland.

The Red Squirrels of Brownsea Island

Breeding and survival

Inevitably many of the red squirrels' activities cover more than one season, and the breeding period is no exception. Males and females reach sexual maturity by the time they are eleven months old, and young females breeding for the first time will have their summer kittens in July.

The breeding season, which is spread over eight to ten months, begins during late winter and early spring; as the gestation period is around thirty eight days, these litters are born during March and April. Some squirrels produce two litters a year, with an average of three kittens in each.

The female is very protective of her young during lactation, but quickly loses interest once they are weaned.

Although the kittens are born with well developed claws and feet, they are blind, deaf and hairless. When they are five weeks old they look more like small versions of adult red squirrels, and by seven weeks old they venture out of the drey, where they would be vulnerable to predators. On the mainland there would be many predators such as foxes, stoats, domestic cats and birds: on Brownsea only the latter applies.

There is about a 70% chance that young red squirrels, which have survived the post weaning period, will not survive the first year: those that do have a good chance of living a few years – three or four being the average span of a squirrel's life.

Ranges and Territories

The red squirrel's range is determined by food availability, and is usually between two and five acres. The ranges overlap, which is why several red squirrels may be seen in close proximity to each other. They guard their patch from other squirrels, which they mark by urinating on it.

Females with young kittens may defend small territories in the area immediately surrounding the breeding drey.

There is probably a hierarchical social structure, with squirrels higher up the scale commanding larger areas.

Squirrels can become agitated if another squirrel's scent is picked up. They rarely fight but flick their tails and make a churring sound, and at times chase each other noisily.

Changing Appearance Throughout the Year

The body fur of the red squirrel is moulted in the spring and autumn. Tail and ear tufts moult only once a year, just before the autumn moult.

The spring moult starts at the head and progresses towards the rear; it is the other way round in the autumn.

Between August and November the summer coat is moulted and a thicker, darker winter one grows. The ear tufts are very prominent: the tail fur is long and thick.

In preparation for the winter the red squirrel needs to gain at least 10% of its body weight if it is to survive the bleak months ahead. By January the fur which has bleached since the moult is now a creamy colour.

9

Food Gathering

Squirrels will eat according to the
season and their environment, their
daily diet depending on where they live.
For two months in the spring pine seed is not
readily available: during this time the red squirrels
feed off young tender buds, leaves and insects.
By May they eat the developing seed in the new
green unripe cones, and from July onwards, the
ripe, brown cones are available
until late winter.
As spring turns into summer, the daily routine
of foraging and storing food takes up much
of the red squirrel's life. Once he has found
buried nuts the squirrel seems to know by
the weight whether or not it contains a
juicy kernel, so does not waste
valuable time and energy
opening dud nuts.
It is fascinating to
watch a squirrel
shaking a hazel
nut, then either
discarding it,
or transferring it
from his paws
to his mouth.

Foraging for most of the year takes place in the tree tops, where they feed on shoots, catkins, sweet chestnuts and cones. The red squirrel prefers a closed canopy, which provides cover and facilitates travel amongst the branches without touching the ground.

During the longer days of summer the red squirrel's activity increases, and with their food consumption becoming greater, the need for an afternoon sleep is crucial: then after emptying their stomachs, they continue to forage once more.

As the long days of summer turn to autumn the activity of the red squirrel is heightened.

Making the most of the autumn seed, they busy themselves until dark with eating and storing food away. Almost all of the red squirrel's waking hours are taken up with these activities.

At this time of year, when tree seed is more freely available, the red squirrels travel further in search of the best food.

Amazingly they can eat various poisonous plants without getting sick.

In Spring before the new generation of green cones are available, intact cones from the previous year's crop become harder to find, and the red squirrels will spend time ground-feeding and searching for windblown cones that have retained their seed. Insects, eggs and young birds also form part of their diet, as well as fungi; particularly Vuilleminia, which during the winter months, when food is scarce, grows beneath the bark of dead or dying oak trees. As well as having excellent vision and sensitive hearing the red squirrel has a good sense of smell, which is important during the winter months in finding buried food, as the squirrel has no memory of where it was hidden.

If they do not store enough nuts away during the autumn, the following months can be difficult, and some red squirrels may die.

Living Accommodation for the Red Squirrel

If it were possible to slice open a drey it would reveal an inner soft lining usually made up of leaves, moss, feathers and shredded grass.

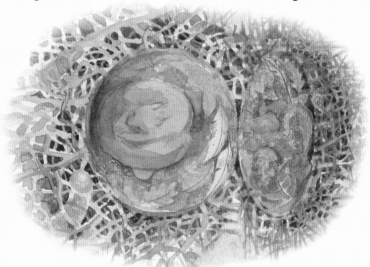

The drey is about 30cm across with the outer waterproof layer constructed of twigs, usually built in a conifer tree at least twenty feet (6 metres) above ground level. Most squirrels have two or three dreys at any one time, which can be very useful during the wintry weather when nests often become wet or uninhabitable.

In spite of weather conditions, many winter dreys will last for several years.

As well as having dreys for a home, the red squirrel also builds dens. As the dens are built in enclosed areas they are harder to find.

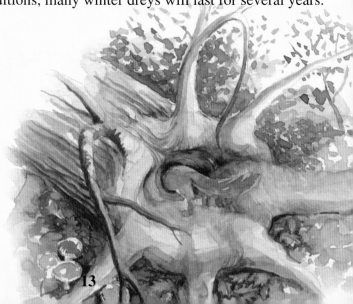

The adventurous squirrel will always be on the lookout for alternative living space.
In recent years the red squirrels on Brownsea have taken to using nestboxes, at first by gnawing larger entrance holes to the bird boxes put up by the National Trust.
In the past few years purpose built squirrel boxes have been erected, forty in total: they are larger versions of bird boxes but with the addition of a little entrance porch.
Nearly all the boxes have been used by the squirrels to some extent, and as many as twenty five have been used for breeding purposes.

Holes in old or dead trees can also be used and enlarged to give variety and choice to the living accommodation of the red squirrel.

Spotting Red Squirrels throughout the Year

Numbers vary annually and throughout the year, peaking in the autumn. The number of squirrels is affected by various factors such as disease and breeding success, the latter being influenced by the food supply, which itself may be determined by the weather.

Original estimates in the 1970s suggested there were between seventy and ninety red squirrels on Brownsea, but more recent surveys have shown there are at least double this number, with a maximum of around two hundred.

Red squirrels can be seen in most wooded parts of the island, but they are wild animals and quite shy. The best time to see the red squirrel is in the morning or late afternoon.

In the autumn look near sweet chestnut and beech trees: they like the nuts these trees produce.

Listen for falling debris from squirrels eating.

Look up: the squirrels live in trees most of the time; try not to make too much noise.

Follow the red squirrel trail.

Look for evidence of squirrels feeding around pine trees: they eat cones in a very distinctive way. Walk quietly.

Red squirrels are active in both summer and winter: they do not hibernate, and need to feed regularly.

During these two seasons there is a marked difference in the times of activities. In the winter months when the hours of daylight are shorter, weather permitting, the red squirrels are active for much of the day: whereas in the summer months with the longer hours of daylight there are two peaks of activities; early morning and evening.

If the weather is severe in the winter months, there may be short spells of inactivity.

Are the Red Squirrels being Conserved on Brownsea?

The National Trust is encouraging natural regeneration of the pine woodlands. The Trust will continue this work on Brownsea as it is essential for the survival of the red squirrels on the island.

Woodland management is vital to maintain the diversity of the age structure of the trees within the woodland, so as to ensure a continuous supply of seed bearing cones.

A large number of trees were destroyed in a fire which swept the island in 1934. Much of the present woodland is of a similar age, springing up since that catastrophic event. Scots pines only begin to produce worthwhile numbers of cones on reaching the age of about twenty years, and cone production peaks in trees aged eighty to ninety years. Trees between these ages also provide the best nest sites.

Other conifer species should be present to help reduce the chance of simultaneous cone crop failure. Over mature trees are retained wherever possible to supply seed for regeneration and provide rotting and holed timber for use by squirrels as den sites.

The rotting timber is also used by other wildlife such as woodpeckers.

Other work by The National Trust includes getting rid of the rhododendron which was brought to the island by the Victorians; although it has pretty flowers, nothing can grow underneath it.

Once the undergrowth is cleared, young pines will grow naturally from seed in the soil.

Part of the aim of the programme of work by The National Trust is to create a Caledonian type landscape, consisting of a fairly open aspect with blocks of pine trees of differing ages, but containing a high concentration of mature trees with reliable cone production, dispersed within areas of heath.

Brownsea Island would once have been covered by heathland, which is a rare and diminishing habitat in southern England: the National Trust has restored areas of heathland on the island.

Fencing is erected around new woodland in order to stop rabbits and deer eating the young trees.

The National Trust also culls some rabbits and deer each year.

If somehow a grey squirrel did get to the island, the policy of The National Trust is to humanely dispose of it as soon as possible.

How can we help?

The National Trust, Dorset Wildlife Trust (DWT), John Lewis Partnership, Scouts and Guides and English Nature all work together to conserve the red squirrel, and you can too!

There are various ways you can help to look after the island and the red squirrels.
You may like to become a volunteer and help the red squirrels directly, or perhaps to make a donation to the red squirrel conservation work.
Volunteers carry out important conservation work and meet every other Sunday throughout the year.
Your admission fee helps and so does membership of the National Trust.
Please visit the island as often as you can.
The National Trust has a full events programme, which includes special guided red squirrel walks in September and October.
There is also a programme of education for visitors to help them understand about red squirrels and what action needs to be taken to protect them.
This includes guided walks, displays and activities for families and school groups.

When you visit Brownsea, the staff at the Visitor Centre and throughout the island will be only too pleased to give you more information.
You will find the island shop full of books and red squirrel souvenirs, and the Villano café has delicious food and drinks.
The DWT and the National Trust are undertaking ongoing conservation work to secure the red squirrel's future on Brownsea Island.

Recently the DWT launched an appeal for people to 'adopt a squirrel', to help raise funds to safeguard their Brownsea Island site. The 'adopt a squirrel' campaign is a great way to raise funds, and has been backed by Sir David Attenborough.

The cost of adopting a squirrel is £15, and includes a certificate, fact sheets, badges and a copy of Beatrix Potter's The Tale of Squirrel Nutkin. For more details on adoption and becoming a volunteer for the DWT, please telephone the DWT on 01305 264620.

For more details on membership or becoming a volunteer for the National Trust, please telephone 01202 707744.

Fascinating Squirrel Facts

The red squirrel's latin name, Sciurus vulgaris goes back to Aristotle, who first named the animal Skiouros or 'shade-tail', from the Greek *skia,* shade and *oura,* tail.

Very occasionally albino red squirrels may be sighted.

The red squirrel's hind legs are extremely powerful, enabling it to leap as much as six metres. The hind foot has a double joint which enables it to hang flat against a tree trunk upside down. The fore legs are much shorter, and act as shock absorbers when the animal lands.

Squirrels are good swimmers and have been known to swim across rivers half a mile wide.

Red squirrels are fully protected in Britain by the Wildlife and Countryside Act (1981), as they are regarded as an endangered species.

It is unlikely that there was a colony of squirrels on Brownsea Island before the mid 1700s, as until then there were far fewer trees on the island than there are today.
There are no records to show how the red squirrels arrived on the island, or when and where they came from.

On Brownsea Island squirrels have been seen to forage in the litter bins and at least one squirrel has learned to tap on the kitchen window of the warden's flat at The Villa when it wants to be fed!

The disease squirrel pox virus is similar to myxomatosis in rabbits. The symptoms are severe swelling around the face, mucus discharge, staggering and finally death for the unfortunate squirrels.
This horrid disease is thought to be stress related.

In the cold weather it has been known for red squirrels to share their dreys with their neighbours.